Science

MATTER

and the

Baseball

Park

WHIZZZZ

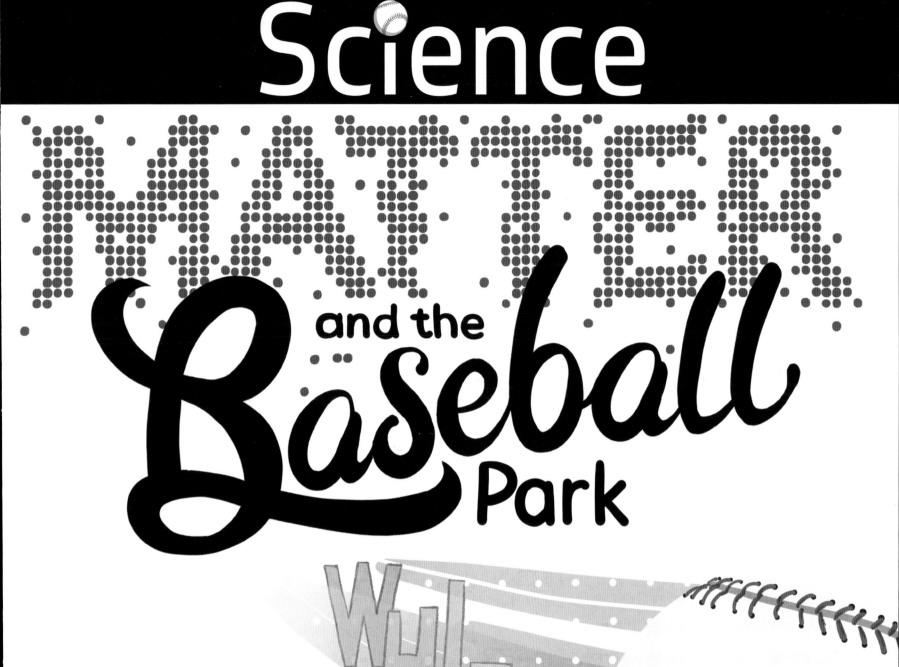

Story by Catherine Ciocchi
Art by Chantelle and Burgen Thorne

GNOME ROAD PUBLISHING
Louisville, Kentucky, USA
www.gnomeroadpublishing.com
Logo designs by Wendy Leach, copyright © 2023
by Gnome Road Publishing

Summary: Science meets baseball in this fast-paced
rhyming story that *zooms* in on all the matter -
whether solid, liquid or gas - that makes up what truly
matters at the ballpark and beyond.

Complimentary classroom materials for use with this
book are available at www.gnomeroadpublishing.com.

ISBN 978-1-957655-02-4 (trade)
ISBN 978-1-957655-10-9 (ebook)

Library of Congress Control Number: 2022939177
LC record available at:
https://lccn.loc.gov/2022939177
Illustrations were rendered by hand in ClipStudio.
The text of this book is set in Soleto font.

First Edition
Manufactured in India

Science
MATTER
and the
Baseball
Park

Story by
Catherine Ciocchi
Art by Chantelle
and Burgen Thorne

For my team that
matters most;
my husband Dave
and my sons
Dave, Nick and Alex.
- CC

To the teachers
and the scientists –
thank you!
- C&B

There's a ballgame today,
and the crowd shuffles in.

PANTHERS   TIGERS

ATTER UP   CONCESSION STAND   SOUTHPAW   Fast Ball   HOME RUN!!   CURVEBALL   Ra

The fans wear team colors and hope for a win.

There's **matter**
that's also a part of the game.

It's all through the ballpark,
but not all the same.

Matter is anything
taking up space.
This is why matter's
all over the place.
The cameraman films
all this matter around,
from the top
of the stands . . .

. . . to the grass
on the ground.

It's game time!
The batter steps up
to the plate.

The pitch is a fastball.
His swing is too late.

Let's look at the matter on instant replay. All matter is different and made its own way.

We'll zoom in on **atoms**. They're very small parts.

They make up all matter
and that's where it starts.

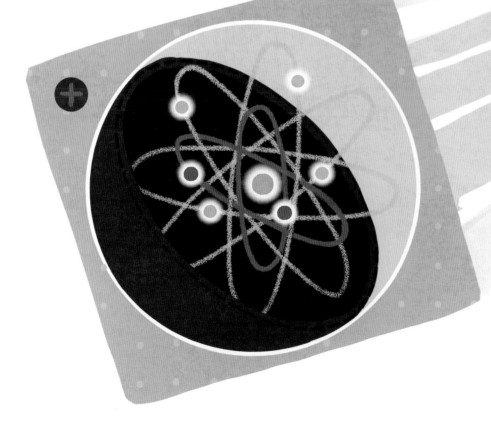

The helmet protecting
the head of the batter,
feels hard to the touch.
It's a **solid** type matter.

The atoms in solids are packed really tight. There's no room to move to the left or the right.

The scoreboard is solid and so is the bat. A jersey is solid, along with a hat.

The kids near the dugout
who hang on the fence,

drink cold **liquid** matter throughout the suspense.

The atoms in liquid
can wiggle with ease.
It pours and it drips
like the hot nacho cheese.

Ice cream that's melted
and anything wet,
slushies are liquid
and yes, even sweat!

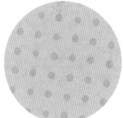

Let's watch as the bat
moves the air, then the ball.
The air is a **gas** with few atoms at all.

The atoms in gas have
more space to move free.
These far apart atoms make
gas hard to see.

WHOOOSH

There's gas in the blimp floating high in the sky, and in the balloons on a string passing by.

The amount of matter is known as the **mass**.

All matter is solid,
or liquid or gas.

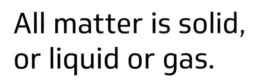

Now back to the action.
The pitcher throws heat.
The bat makes a CRACK sound.
The crowd's on their feet.

The noise from the stands is a gasp, then a cheer.

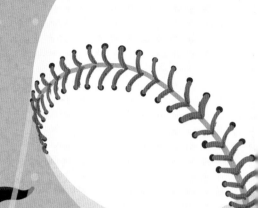

That ball, we call matter, is way OUTTA HERE!!